# TOP 10 COLLEGE FOOTBALL COACHES

Ron Knapp

## SPORTS TOP 10

**Enslow Publishers, Inc.**

40 Industrial Road          PO Box 38
Box 398                     Aldershot
Berkeley Heights, NJ 07922  Hants GU12 6BP
USA                         UK

http://www.enslow.com

**Library of Congress Cataloging-in-Publication Data**

Knapp, Ron.
    Top 10 college football coaches / Ron Knapp.
        p. cm. — (Sports top 10)
    Includes bibliographical references (p. 46) and index.
    Summary: Profiles ten celebrated college football coaches, including Paul
"Bear" Bryant, Knute Rockne, and Bud Wilkinson.
    ISBN 0-7660-1073-2
    1. Football coaches—United States—Biography—Juvenile literature.
    2. Football coaches—Rating of—United States—Juvenile literature.
    [1. Football coaches.] I. Title. II. Series.
GV939.A1K583  1999
796.332'63'092273—dc21
    [B]                                   98-25728
                                             CIP
                                            AC

Printed in the United States of America

10 9 8 7 6 5 4 3 2 1

**To Our Readers:**
All Internet addresses in this book were active and appropriate when we
went to press. Any comments or suggestions can be sent by e-mail to
Comments@enslow.com or to the address on the back cover.

**Illustration Credits:** AP/Wide World Photos, 13, 22, 25, 33, 35, 37; College
Football Hall of Fame, 7, 9, 11, 27, 29, 30, 38, 41, 42, 45; © Mitchell Layton,
14, 17, 19, 21.

**Cover Illustration:** © Mitchell Layton

**Cover Description:** Head Coach Joe Paterno of the Penn State
Nittany Lions

**Interior Design:** Richard Stalzer

# CONTENTS

# Introduction

THE FIRST AMERICAN COLLEGE FOOTBALL GAME was played November 6, 1869. There were twenty-five men on each team. None of them wore uniforms, helmets, or pads, just everyday clothing. The ball could only be moved by kicking it. Final score: Rutgers 6, Princeton 4.

The first important rules change allowed players to grab the ball and run with it. At first they followed a mob of their teammates who tried to clear a path by punching their way through the opposition.

A few years later, players were allowed to pass the ball. At first, they just lobbed it high into the air, hoping a teammate could run under it. Then, they began throwing hard, spiral passes at their receivers.

New rules outlawed clipping, holding, piling on, and interference. Play did not begin until the center snapped the ball to the quarterback. Instead of having their teams advance downfield like a mob, coaches developed formations. When three backs stood side by side behind their quarterback, the T-formation was born. The split T moved the players apart; the double wingback put them on opposite sides of the field.

Along with formations came a variety of plays. Coaches taught their quarterbacks to hand the ball off or lateral it to their backs. Sometimes a back had the choice, or option, of either running the ball himself or throwing it to a teammate downfield.

Football became the favorite sport on college campuses. Students flocked to the games. So did the alumni; older people who had already graduated from the colleges. Huge stadiums were built to hold thousands of people.

Two of the coaches in this book, Amos Alonzo Stagg and Pop Warner, were there almost at the beginning. Their coaching careers began in the nineteenth century. Knute Rockne became an incredibly popular personality in the 1920s. Bear Bryant, Woody Hayes, and Bud Wilkinson were riding high in the 1950s and beyond. Eddie Robinson's career, which just ended, spanned more than fifty years. Barry Switzer moved to the pros in 1994. Tom Osborne retired from Nebraska after the 1997 season, with his team having just won a share of the national championship. Joe Paterno continues to direct Penn State, one of America's top teams.

There have been many great college football coaches. Perhaps you can think of some that are not on *our* list. We feel that together, these ten coaches have helped make college football the wonderful, exciting game it is today.

# CAREER STATISTICS

| Coach | Years | Schools | Wins | Losses | Ties | Pct. |
|---|---|---|---|---|---|---|
| PAUL "BEAR" BRYANT | 38 | Maryland, Kentucky, Texas A&M, Alabama | 323 | 85 | 17 | .780 |
| WOODY HAYES | 33 | Denison, Miami-OH, Ohio State | 238 | 72 | 10 | .759 |
| TOM OSBORNE | 25 | Nebraska | 255 | 49 | 3 | .836 |
| JOE PATERNO | 33 | Penn State | 307 | 80 | 3 | .791 |
| EDDIE ROBINSON | 54 | Grambling | 408 | 165 | 15 | .707 |
| KNUTE ROCKNE | 13 | Notre Dame | 105 | 12 | 5 | .881 |
| AMOS ALONZO STAGG | 57 | Springfield College, Chicago, Pacific | 314 | 199 | 35 | .605 |
| BARRY SWITZER | 16 | Oklahoma | 157 | 29 | 4 | .837 |
| POP WARNER | 44 | Georgia, Cornell, Carlisle, Pittsburgh, Stanford, Temple | 319 | 106 | 32 | .733 |
| BUD WILKINSON | 17 | Oklahoma | 145 | 29 | 4 | .826 |

Statistics through 1998 season.

# PAUL "BEAR" BRYANT

**WHEN HE WAS GROWING UP** in rural Arkansas, Paul "Bear" Bryant said, "All I had was football. I hung on as though it were life or death, which it was."[1]

His classmates made fun of the clothes he wore and the old mule-driven wagon in which he rode to school. "He never forgot the ones who belittled him. . . ." said his sister Louise. "He was determined to show them he was made of something special."[2]

Bryant was a big tough kid, but he did not seem to be much of an athlete. After school he worked at a grain store. "If he didn't tear it up or mess it up," said his boss, "he fell over it. That's how clumsy Paul was."[3]

The boy might have been awkward, but he was strong. When a touring carnival offered a dollar a minute to anybody who would wrestle a bear, fourteen-year-old Bryant jumped on stage. "I got the bear pinned, holdin' on real tight." The boy planned on keeping the animal down and earning lots of money, but "the bear finally shook loose and the next thing I knew his muzzle had come off."[4] When the bear bit his head, Bryant jumped off the stage, ending the fight. After that, his friends called him Bear.

When Bryant was in eighth grade, his school's football coach invited him to play. The game was simple, he told the boy. You find the man with the ball, then "you go down there and try to kill him."[5] Soon he had cleats screwed in to his only pair of shoes. In 1930, his senior year, he led the Fordyce Redbugs to the Arkansas State Championship.

Bear moved on to the University of Alabama, where he played right end. In 1935, he fractured his shinbone early

After stops at Maryland, Kentucky, and Texas A&M, Paul "Bear" Bryant coached the Alabama Crimson Tide for twenty-four years.

PAUL "BEAR" BRYANT

in a game against Mississippi State. After sitting out a quarter, he returned to finish the game. He did not get a cast until two days later. Five days after that, he threw down his crutches, and the doctor removed the cast just before a big game against Tennessee. He quickly caught a pass that set up the Crimson Tide's first touchdown, then grabbed another before lateraling to Riley Smith, who scored another. Alabama won, 25–0.

When he became a college coach, Bryant expected his players to be just as tough as he was. His teams worked so hard at practice, one athlete said, that when they were finished, "You had to lay on the floor for thirty minutes before you had the strength to undress and shower."[6]

Bryant had his greatest coaching success at his old school, the University of Alabama, where his team won national championships in 1964, 1965, 1973, 1978, and 1979. In the 1970s, the Crimson Tide became the first college team ever to win one hundred games in a decade.

His victories kept piling up until 1981, when he tied Amos Alonzo Stagg's total of 314 Division I college wins. Then the Crimson Tide ran into the Auburn Tigers. The first half went poorly, so Bryant told his team: "You're acting like you're playin' your little brothers, or something. Like you're afraid you're going to get hurt, or hurt *them*."[7]

Alabama still trailed, 17–14, with two and a half minutes left. From the Auburn 38, quarterback Walter Lewis faked a hand-off to his fullback, then fired a bullet to Jess Bendross, who crossed the goal line to put the Crimson Tide ahead for good. Bear finally got his 315th victory, 28–17.

As he grew older, Bryant was repeatedly asked when he planned to retire. "Quit coaching?" he yelled. "I'd croak in a week."[8]

But Bear finally quit after a 21–15 victory over Illinois. A month later he died of a heart attack.

## PAUL "BEAR" BRYANT

BORN: September 11, 1913, Moro Bottom, Arkansas.

DIED: January 26, 1983, Tuscaloosa, Alabama.

COLLEGE: University of Alabama.

COLLEGE TEAMS COACHED: University of Maryland, 1945; University of Kentucky, 1946–1953; Texas A & M, 1954–1957; University of Alabama, 1958–1982.

HONORS/AWARDS: Led teams to five national titles: 1961, 1964, 1965, 1978, 1979; AFCA Coach of the Year, 1961, 1971, 1973; College Football Hall of Fame, 1986.

RECORDS: Has won more games than any other coach at Division I-A level, 323.

Bryant is carried off the field on the shoulders of his players after a big win. Alabama won or shared five national titles with Bryant at the helm.

**Internet Address**

http://www.bamafan.com/bryant.htm

# WOODY HAYES

**WHEN HE WAS MAD**—and that was often—Woody Hayes might have been the angriest man on earth.

If a player or assistant coach made a mistake, if he did not get the report or equipment he wanted, or if the Ohio State Buckeyes (OSU) got a bad break, Hayes exploded. Sometimes he threw things like water pitchers, a downs marker, or his briefcase. Players got used to seeing him rip caps off his head and tear them to shreds. He also tore off wristwatches, threw them to the field, then stomped them to bits.

Once he raised his eyeglasses over his head and crushed them in his bare hands. The broken glass cut his hands, and blood flowed down his arms. Another time at a meeting, he doubled up his fists and began to scream. "Woody took those two clenched fists," said an assistant coach, "and smashed himself high alongside both cheeks, obviously as hard as he could."[1] The next day he had a pair of black eyes.

Why did he blow his cool? "When I explode," he explained, "I'm telling this: 'The only reason I'm mad is because I know you can do better. You can do more.'"[2]

Hayes's tactics seemed to work. For twenty-eight years, the Buckeyes had one of the most successful teams in the nation, winning 205 games, losing 68, and tying 10.

Some of Hayes's biggest games came against the opponent he hated the most—the Michigan Wolverines. In 1954, with the score tied 7–7, Michigan had a first down at the OSU 4-yard line. For four straight plays, the Wolverines sent a fullback smashing into the Ohio State line. Two yards. One yard. Two feet. Then, the Buckeyes stopped him

WOODY HAYES

Woody Hayes coached the Ohio State Buckeyes from 1951 to 1978, winning three national titles.

six inches from the goal line. Ohio State wound up with a 21–7 victory, and Woody Hayes wound up in the shower with his clothes on, tossed there by his happy players. OSU won the national championship that season.

In 1970, the Wolverines and Buckeyes were undefeated when they met. Hayes's players were ready. They raced madly onto the field, growling, screaming, and punching the air. "Those guys just aren't sane," said a reporter. "I wouldn't want to be a Michigan football player today."[3]

On the kickoff, the Michigan kick returner was blasted simultaneously by three OSU tacklers. The ball popped loose, and the Buckeyes were on their way. When it was over, they had a 20–9 victory.

Throughout his career, Woody usually relied on his "three yards and a cloud of dust" offensive strategy. He figured his teams were tough enough to grind out yardage on the ground, slowly working their way to a touchdown. It was not flashy, but it worked.

Hayes's coaching career came to an abrupt end late in the 1978 Gator Bowl when a Clemson player intercepted a pass, insuring a 17–15 Ohio State defeat. Hayes's anger got the best of him, and he punched the player. Within a few days, he was fired.

Ohio State fans remember not the temper, but the brilliant coach who loved his players. When his players were in trouble or had problems, many of them lived with Hayes and his wife, Anne.

After graduating, his players stayed in touch. Many times their old coach quietly helped them—with advice, assistance in landing a job, or even money for operations.

Matt Snell, a Buckeye star, said, "We always had the feeling that Woody wasn't the kind who was through with you when you played your last game for him."[4]

# WOODY HAYES

BORN: February 14, 1913, Clifton, Ohio.

DIED: March 12, 1987, Upper Arlington, Ohio.

COLLEGE: Denison University.

COLLEGE TEAMS COACHED: Denison University 1946–1948;
University of Miami-Ohio, 1949–1950; Ohio State University,
1951–1978.

HONORS/AWARDS: Led teams to three national titles: 1954, 1957,
1968; AFCA Coach of the Year, 1957; FWAA Coach of the
Year, 1957, 1968, 1975; College Football Hall of Fame,
1983.

Hayes led Ohio State to four Rose Bowl victories.

**Internet Address**

http://www.buckeyezone.com/tradition.html

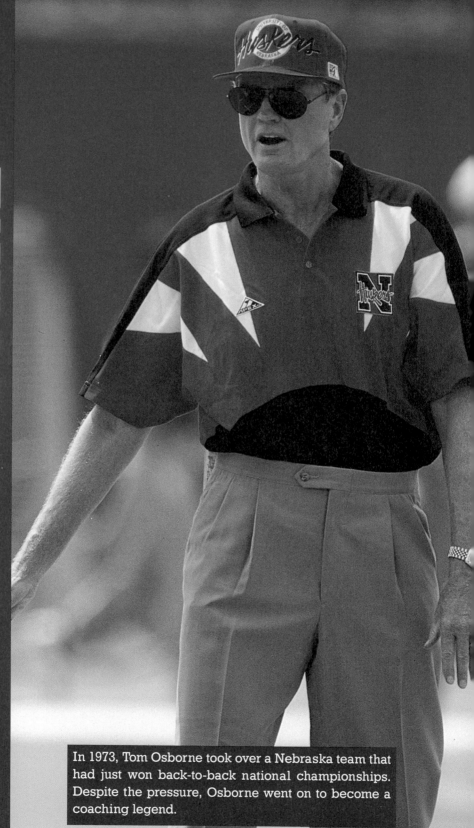

**TOM OSBORNE**

In 1973, Tom Osborne took over a Nebraska team that had just won back-to-back national championships. Despite the pressure, Osborne went on to become a coaching legend.

EVEN WHEN HE WAS GROWING UP in Hastings, Nebraska, Tom Osborne was a shy, quiet person. Since he did not like to talk, his high school classmates jokingly gave him the nickname "Yak." Decades later, when he had become one of the most famous coaches in the nation, surrounded by dozens of reporters and thousands of fans, he said, "There are times when I'd like to evaporate."[1]

In the early 1990s, one of the things reporters always seemed to ask him about was the national championship. The University of Nebraska had won back-to-back titles in 1971 and 1972, just before Osborne took over as head coach. For twenty-one years after that, even though they won at least nine games a year, the Cornhuskers were never No. 1.

Sure, they came close—many times. At the 1984 Orange Bowl, they lost a heartbreaking 31–30 decision—and the national title—to Miami when Osborne chose to go for a last-minute two-point conversion. It failed. In two other seasons, 1981 and 1993, Nebraska also lost the top spot by losing the Orange Bowl. Late-season defeats at the hands of Oklahoma in 1975, 1984, and 1987 kept the Cornhuskers from being No. 1 or No. 2 going into the bowl games. It was beginning to look as if Osborne's teams would never get the big win they needed to take the top spot.

Joe Paterno, the Penn State coach, defended his friend: "To win a national championship, you've got to have a little luck, and Tom has had no luck at all."[2]

The quiet coach got tired of all the talk. "Our obsession with Number One in this country tends to drive us toward the conclusion that you have to reach the top of the hill," he said, "and everybody else is a loser."[3]

The 1995 Orange Bowl looked like the same old story. Miami jumped to a 17–7 lead. Then the Cornhuskers got tough. The defense held Miami to minus 37 yards in the final period while the offense tied the game. Then, with 2:46 left, fullback Cory Schlesinger scored to give Nebraska a 24–17 victory—and the national title. "This is the greatest moment of my life because nobody deserves it more than Tom Osborne," said Zach Wiegert, a Nebraska lineman. "The man perseveres, and we persevered tonight. This one is special."[4]

So was the next one. Osborne's team sewed up their second straight national championship one year later by destroying Florida in the Fiesta Bowl, 62–24. By then, the Cornhuskers were clearly recognized as the dominant college team in the country. Over three seasons (1993–95), their record was 36–1.

Osborne has never minded talking about the problems faced by today's young people: "We have several kids on our team who essentially have no parents and haven't had parental support since they were ten, eleven years old. I think of the cultural environment—the messages kids get from TV and some of the music they listen to. . . ."[5]

To help young people deal with their problems, Osborne works as a Sunday school teacher and has been involved in the Fellowship of Christian Athletes. He and his wife, Nancy, developed the Husker Teammates program to match his football players with local junior high school students.

Osborne retired with 255 victories. In his final game, the 1997 Orange Bowl, the Cornhuskers ripped No. 3 Tennessee, 42–17, to clinch a share of the national title. In his last three seasons, Osborne's teams were 60–3.

Why did he retire? "I think it's wise to back off before you leave feet first or somebody tells you it's time to go."[6]

## TOM OSBORNE

BORN: February 23, 1937, Hastings, Nebraska.

COLLEGE: Hastings College, University of Nebraska-Lincoln.

COLLEGE TEAMS COACHED: University of Nebraska, 1973–1997.

HONORS/AWARDS: Led teams to three national titles: 1994, 1995,
1997; AFCA Coach of the Year, 1994.

With an eye on the action, Osborne thinks about his next move.
Osborne retired after the 1997 season, having won three national
championships in his last four years.

**Internet Address**

http://www.sportingnews.com/cfootball/articles/19971224/34246.html

# JOE PATERNO

JOE PATERNO'S PHILOSOPHY SURPRISES a lot of people. "We're trying to win football games . . .," he said, "but I don't want it to ruin our lives if we lose . . . I tell the kids who come here to play, enjoy yourselves."[1]

Paterno's attitude has not kept his Penn State teams from working hard—or from winning. With less than two minutes to go in the 1968 Orange Bowl, the Nittany Lions trailed, 14–7. Under tremendous defensive pressure, quarterback Chuck Burkhart heaved a 47-yard pass to Bobby Campbell, who brought the ball to the Kansas 3-yard line. Two plays later, Penn State had a touchdown. Instead of playing it safe with a kick attempt, Paterno sent Campbell off tackle. The run was good, and the Nittany Lions won, 15–14.

Going into the second game of the 1970 season, Paterno's team had a thirty-one-game winning streak, the longest in the nation. When they were clobbered by Colorado, 41–13, the Nittany Lions did not pout or complain. The coach heard the cheers for his opponents and told his players, "Listen to them—let them have their glory. We've had our share."[2]

Paterno has usually relied on a strong running game, but sometimes his strategy surprises opponents. With 1:37 remaining in the 1983 Sugar Bowl against Georgia, Penn State led, 27–23. The Nittany Lions had the ball in a third-and-three situation. A first down would put the game on ice. Almost everybody—including his assistants—expected him to call for a run. But his quarterback, Todd Blackledge, said, "I think we can throw it for a first down." As Paterno

JOE PATERNO

Joe Paterno led the Penn State Nittany Lions to a top twenty ranking each year from 1993 to 1998.

explained later, "My gut believed him." He told his quarter-back, "Throw it."[3]

The pass was good for 6 yards. The Nittany Lions had the first down, the victory, an undefeated season, and their first national championship. Another Paterno team, the 1986 squad, also finished the season No. 1.

Not all the coach's decisions went that well. In 1988, Pitt led Penn State, 14–7, midway through the last quarter. The Nittany Lions had possession—fourth and two at the Pitt 22-yard line. Should he let his team go for the first down, then try to score a touchdown and the two-point conversion for a victory? Paterno played it safe and went for the field goal—which missed. His team did not score again.

"You played hard tonight . . .," the coach told his players after the game. "You weren't coached well. I didn't give you the chance to win the game, and I want to tell you I'm very sorry."[4]

For over three decades now, Joe Paterno has been a familiar sight, pacing the Penn State sidelines in his customary get-up—black shoes, white athletic socks, and rolled-up dark pants. Several professional teams in the National Football League have attempted to lure him away from the Nittany Lions.

In 1973, he almost signed a $1.3 million contract with the Boston Patriots. "In the end," he said, "I didn't feel I should leave a job where I had been happy, where I have made so many friends. It's a good atmosphere . . . I have five kids and this is the perfect place to raise them."[5]

# JOE PATERNO

BORN: December 21, 1926, Brooklyn, New York.

COLLEGE: Brown University.

COLLEGE TEAMS COACHED: Penn State University, 1966– .

HONORS/AWARDS: Led teams to two national titles: 1982, 1986. AFCA
Coach of the Year, 1968, 1978, 1982, 1986; FWAA Coach of
the Year, 1978, 1982, 1986.

Paterno has won more bowl games than any other Division I-A
head coach.

## Internet Address

http://www.bigten.org/sports/football/teams/ppb/coaches.htm

EDDIE ROBINSON

Giving some last-minute instructions, Eddie Robinson gets Grambling ready for a big game.

IN 1941, TWENTY-ONE-YEAR-OLD Eddie Robinson became football coach at Louisiana Negro Normal and Industrial School. Most of the students at the African-American college were young women studying to be teachers. There were only seventy male students. Robinson's pay was $16 a week. At the time, southern African Americans could only attend segregated schools.

Fifty-six years later, the school's name had long since been changed to Grambling State University. The team played its games in Eddie Robinson Stadium. Robinson's Grambling Tigers had long been the strongest squad in African-American college football. More than two hundred of his players have signed with the National Football League. The first African-American quarterback to play on a winning Super Bowl team is a Grambling graduate, Doug Williams. When Robinson retired in 1997, he was the winningest coach in the history of college or professional football. Williams became his replacement.

Robinson's career record was 408–165–15. His second team, in 1942, went 9–0. In the process, his defense shut out every opponent.

One of his greatest victories came fifty years later, in a game against Southern University. After three quarters, Grambling was behind, 27–16. Robinson told his men to keep plugging; they could still win. Finally, with just thirty-six seconds left, quarterback Alex Perkins popped over the goal line from three yards out. The Tigers won, 30–27, earning them a spot in the Heritage Bowl, which they won six weeks later.

Robinson also stressed the importance of education. The bell in the football dormitory rang at 6:30 A.M. "I personally ring that big bell every school day," the coach said. "I want to make certain every player gets up in time to make their 8 A.M. class."[1] Players who missed morning classes were punished with one hundred pushups. Freshman athletes were required to attend an etiquette class. "It's important for young men to be courteous in public and know how to dress. . . . We think we're good role models for young people."[2]

When laws were passed in the 1960s outlawing segregation, African Americans could attend formerly all-white schools. The nation's top African-American athletes no longer had to attend African-American colleges like Grambling, but many of them did. They wanted to play for the man they called "Coach Rob."

Some of the modern players disappointed Robinson. "They don't want to work," he said. "They want to go straight to the NFL, and they don't even have the grades to stay in school. And they don't have the talent."[3]

When he was forced by the college to resign in 1997, he said he was not bitter. "I have had one job, one wife. I had a chance to coach some of the finest players who ever played the game. I've been working at Grambling for fifty-six years and my paycheck has never been late."[4]

Eddie Robinson was never one to brag. When he won his 400th game on October 7, 1995, he did not want to talk about himself: "I wish I could cut up all of these victories into four hundred pieces and give them to all of the players and assistant coaches I've had."[5]

After his last game on November 29, 1997, he said, "These fifty-six years, I've been about the happiest man in the world."[6]

## EDDIE ROBINSON

BORN: February 3, 1919, Jackson, Louisiana.

COLLEGE: Leland College.

COLLEGE TEAMS COACHED: Grambling State University, 1941–1942, 1945–1997.

HONORS/AWARDS: Led Grambling to eight national black college titles; won more games than any coach in college history.

For fifty-six years, Eddie Robinson was the head coach at Grambling State University.

**Internet Address**

http://www.eddierobinson.org

# KNUTE ROCKNE

DURING THE SUMMER OF 1913, Gus Dorais and Knute Rockne worked in a restaurant at Cedar Point, a resort in Ohio. To relax, they threw a football back-and-forth on the beach. Up until that time, most coaches thought the only way to move the ball was to run. All that changed that fall when Dorais completed twelve passes, most of them to Rockne, as Notre Dame, a small, little-known college in Indiana, upset Army, one of the nation's toughest teams, 35–13.

Five years later, Rockne became Notre Dame's head coach. After going 3–1–2, his team had two undefeated seasons. The coach became a familiar figure on the sidelines, sitting in a canvas chair as he directed his players.

Rockne's "Notre Dame shift" was soon copied by teams all over the country. Just before the ball was snapped, his four offensive backs moved together in the backfield to confuse the opposition.

But it was not tactics alone that made the Fighting Irish great; it was Rockne's ability to motivate his players. Before a big game in 1922 against Georgia Tech, he read his players a telegram he said was from his four-year-old son, Billy, who was very sick in the hospital: "Please win this game for my Daddy." The message did the trick. "We tore that Georgia Tech team apart and beat 'em, 13–3," said Don Miller, one of his players. "They never had a chance."[1] The team did not find out until they got back to Indiana that Billy was fine. Rockne had made up the whole story.

It was the words of sportswriter Grantland Rice who made sure Notre Dame's 1924 backfield would always be

More than a football coach, Knute Rockne was an American sports legend. The Postal Service printed this stamp in his honor.

KNUTE ROCKNE

remembered. Since they destroyed their foes, he compared them to the "Four Horsemen of the Apocalypse" from the Bible—Famine, Pestilence, Destruction, and Death. His article began, "Outlined against a blue-gray October sky, the Four Horsemen rode again."[2]

In 1925, Notre Dame trailed Northwestern, 10–0, at halftime. "Rock" was disappointed—and angry. "I do know a lousy, gutless performance . . ." he yelled. "You've quit out there—and if you can quit, so can I!"[3] Then he stormed out of the locker room and took a seat in the stands. The embarrassed Fighting Irish stormed back for a 13–10 victory.

Rockne gave his most famous pep talk in 1928, the year his team went 5–4–0, his worst record. Without great talent, Notre Dame had to face Army, still a very tough team. Rockne asked his players to remember George Gipp, a star on one of his early teams, who had died in 1920. The coach said the dying athlete had told him, "Rock, someday when things look real tough for Notre Dame, ask the boys to go out there and win one for me." Then Rockne added, "This is the time. It's up to you."[4] The Irish upset Army, 12–6, and "Win one for the Gipper!" became a Notre Dame battle cry.

Rockne's next two teams were undefeated. By then, he was one of the most popular men in the country. His magazine articles and newspaper columns were read by millions. Hundreds of schools bought football equipment bearing his name. He earned thousands of dollars giving speeches all over the country. When he was offered $50,000 in 1931 to play the part of a football coach in a movie, he decided to fly to California to finalize the deal.[5]

On March 31, 1931, his plane crashed, and Knute Rockne died. He was only forty-three.

# KNUTE ROCKNE

BORN: March 4, 1888, Voss, Norway.

DIED: March 31, 1931, Chase County, Kansas.

COLLEGE: Notre Dame University.

COLLEGE TEAMS COACHED: Notre Dame University, 1918–1930.

HONORS/AWARDS: Led teams to three national titles: 1924, 1929, 1930; College Football Hall of Fame, 1951; highest winning percentage in the history of Division I-A, .881.

Perhaps trying to land a big recruit, Knute Rockne explains his coaching method to baseball legend Babe Ruth.

**Internet Address**

http://home.sol.no/~birgerro/krtribute.htm

**AMOS ALONZO STAGG**

Amos Alonzo Stagg was one of football's greatest innovators. He invented the tackling dummy and many offensive plays that are still in use today.

# AMOS ALONZO STAGG

**AMOS ALONZO STAGG WAS** such a fine baseball pitcher at Yale University that the New York Giants offered him a contract. Stagg refused; he wanted no part of a sport that allowed alcoholic drinks to be sold at its games.

Stagg was also a star end on the 1888 Yale football team, which outscored its opponents 704–0. A year later he was named to the first All-America team.

After college, Stagg gave up dreams of being a minister when he realized he was a poor preacher. "I stammered terribly," he said.[1] He became a player-coach at the YMCA in Springfield, Massachusetts. One of his football players was James Naismith, the man who would later invent basketball.

In 1892, Stagg became head football coach at the University of Chicago. At first, since he had only thirteen players, he would sometimes suit up and play. Two years later, he surprised fans by traveling all the way to California for a game against Stanford. One of the student managers for the home team was Herbert Hoover, who would later become president of the United States. Chicago won, 28–0.

During his forty-one seasons as Chicago's head coach, Stagg's ideas changed the sport of football. He invented the huddle, reverse play, onside kick, and he was the first to design plays that sent a man in motion. His players were the first to earn varsity letters, use a tackling dummy, and wear numbers on their uniforms. Stagg wrote the first book about football plays and strategy.

While he was in Chicago, the coach worked on other sports as well. His athletes were probably the first to slide head-first in baseball and to practice in batting cages. Stagg came up with the idea of troughs to catch the overflow water from swimming pools. He also organized the first nationwide high school basketball tournament and coached the first intercollegiate five-on-five basketball game.

Even though the University of Chicago was much smaller than many of the schools it played against, Stagg's football teams won the Western Conference (now the Big Ten) title seven times. Four of his teams were undefeated.

When he was seventy, in 1932, Stagg retired from Chicago, but he did not stop coaching. For the next fourteen seasons, he was head coach at the College of the Pacific. In 1943, after his team upset UCLA and the University of California (Berkeley), the eighty-one-year-old was named Coach of the Year. In 1947, he signed a ten-year contract to help his son, Alonzo, Jr., at Susquehanna University. "Formally, he was my assistant," said the younger man. "Practically, he was in charge."[2] Stagg's last job was at Stockton (California) Junior College as a kicking coach in 1960. By then, he was ninety-eight years old.

Amos Alonzo Stagg always thought coaching was much more than just calling plays and winning games. "Our profession is one of the noblest and perhaps the most far reaching in building up the manhood of our country," he wrote in 1927. "Not to drink liquors, not to gamble, not to smoke, not to swear, not to use smutty language, not to tell dirty stories. . . . All these should be the ideals of the athletic coach."[3]

# Amos Alonzo Stagg

BORN: August 16, 1862, West Orange, New Jersey.

DIED: March 17, 1965, Stockton, California.

COLLEGE: Yale University.

COLLEGE TEAMS COACHED: Springfield College, 1890–1891; University of Chicago, 1892–1932; College of the Pacific, 1933–1946.

HONORS/AWARDS: Led University of Chicago to national championship, 1905; AFCA Coach of the Year, 1943; inducted into College Football Hall of Fame as player, 1889, as coach, 1951; inducted into Naismith Memorial Basketball Hall of Fame, 1959.

On the sideline with his Pacific players, Amos Alonzo Stagg follows the action.

# BARRY SWITZER

BARRY SWITZER NEVER HAD ANY DOUBT about what he wanted to do at the University of Oklahoma. "I'll tell you what, people," he said at his first practice as head coach. "The greatest reward in football is winning. That's why they have scoreboards."[1]

Oklahoma was a scoring machine when Switzer was in charge. Using the wishbone formation, his teams led the nation in rushing in 1974, 1977, 1978, 1981, and 1986. The Sooners were an exciting, explosive team.

One of Switzer's first star running backs was "Little Joe" Washington. Against Missouri in 1975, Oklahoma was behind, 27–20, with four minutes to go. The Sooners had the ball, fourth and one, at their own 24-yard line. Everybody in the stadium figured Switzer would call for a quarterback sneak, but he told his quarterback, Steve Davis, to fade back, then pitch the ball to Washington. "You make sure Joe gets the ball."[2]

"Little Joe" took the pitch and took off. Seventy-one yards later, he was in the end zone with his team down by one, 27–26. Switzer was not interested in a tie. He told Davis to run the same play for the two-point conversion attempt. Washington took the pitch, jumped over the Missouri line, and gave the Sooners a 28–27 win.

Switzer's teams had already won a pair of national championships when they met Ohio State, coached by Woody Hayes, in 1977. After blowing a 20–0 lead, they were behind 28–26 with three seconds left. Switzer sent in Uwe von Schamann to attempt a 41-yard field goal. The Buckeye crowd screamed, "Block that kick!" but they fell silent

Studying the play on the field, Barry Switzer plans his next call.

**BARRY SWITZER**

when the ball sailed over the goal post. The coach called the 29–28 victory "one of the greatest things I ever saw or participated in."[3]

Another Sooners kicker saved the day in 1983 against Jimmy Johnson's Oklahoma State Cowboys. Trailing 20–18 late in the game, Tim Lashar punched an onside kick off the helmet of a Cowboys lineman, and Oklahoma recovered. A few plays later, Lashar booted a field goal, resulting in a 21–20 victory.

Switzer bumped into Joe Paterno and Penn State for the first time in the 1986 Orange Bowl. Early in the game, the Nittany Lions contained Oklahoma's defense and scored a touchdown of their own. Switzer responded by calling for a long pass from Jamelle Holieway to Keith Jackson. It was good for 71 yards and a touchdown. Four Lashar field goals then helped the Sooners coast to a 25–10 win that clinched Switzer's third national championship.

Throughout his career, Switzer had to defend himself and his team against alleged recruiting violations and steroid abuse. By 1989, the charges had gotten even more serious. The NCAA put the Oklahoma program on probation for a series of violations. There had been a rape and a shooting in the football dormitory. His quarterback was arrested for selling cocaine. University officials asked Switzer to resign.

Switzer was bitter. "I never would have dreamed that . . . these lies would have forced me to resign one of the best head-coaching jobs in the country."[4] Switzer coached the Dallas Cowboys in the NFL, from 1994 to 1997. He led them to victory in Super Bowl XXX.

## BARRY SWITZER

BORN: October 5, 1937, Crossett, Arkansas.

COLLEGE: University of Arkansas.

COLLEGE TEAMS COACHED: University of Oklahoma, 1973–1988.

HONORS/AWARDS: Led teams to three national titles: 1974, 1975, 1985; led Dallas Cowboys to victory in Super Bowl XXX.

Despite his success, Switzer was forced to leave the University of Oklahoma.

**Internet Address**

http://oufans.cwis.net/barry.html

**POP WARNER**

Pop Warner was one of college football's pioneers. He is credited with inventing such things as the blocking sled and the single- and double-wing formations.

# POP WARNER

**WHEN GLENN S. WARNER ENROLLED** at Cornell University in 1892, he was already twenty-one years old. His freshman classmates, who were still teenagers, nicknamed him Pop. He was a star guard on the Big Red football team. For two years, he was also Cornell's heavyweight boxing champion.

After graduating from law school, instead of becoming a lawyer, Warner decided to be a football coach. For thirteen years, he coached at the Carlisle Indian Institute, a vocational school in Pennsylvania. His star player was Jim Thorpe. It was Pop who convinced Thorpe to return to school in 1911 after dropping out two years before. That extra season of football helped prepare Thorpe for the 1912 Olympics, where he won gold medals in the pentathlon and decathlon. "You, sir," the King of Sweden told Thorpe, "are the greatest athlete in the world."[1]

In a game against Harvard in 1903, Pop came up with one of football's greatest trick plays. Jimmy Johnson caught a kickoff and was quickly surrounded by his Carlisle teammates. Charley Dillon, a quick runner, bent over so Johnson could shove the ball inside the back of his jersey. Then the team stretched out in a long line and ran toward the goal line. Of course, the Harvard players could not see who had the ball. Dillon easily made it to the end zone for a touchdown.

Warner moved to the University of Pittsburgh in 1915 and coached the Panthers to three straight undefeated seasons.

In 1924, he became head coach at Stanford University.

His team was matched against Knute Rockne's Notre Dame squad for the 1925 Rose Bowl. Unfortunately, Warner's best player, the great back Ernie Nevers, could barely walk because of leg injuries. "Pop got some aluminum, shears, and a hammer and went to work," Nevers said. The coach made a movable brace that his player wore under a layer of tape. For a finishing touch, he attached an inner tube to Nevers's heel, then taped the other end above his knee.[2] The strange device allowed the Stanford star to practice. He was in good enough shape for the game that he led all rushers, but the Fighting Irish won, 27–10.

During his forty-four years as a coach, Warner's innovations made college football safer and more exciting. His players were the first to wear molded pads. Nobody had seen the single- and double-wing formations until Warner's players tried them. He invented the sliding blocking sled and the three-point stance.

Warner had other ideas for rule changes that he hoped would open up the game and result in more scoring. Why have a second-half kickoff? Pop said just put it where it had been at the end of the first half. To promote long returns, he wanted defensive players to stay at least five yards away from the return man until he caught the ball.

Of course, these ideas were never fully adopted, but Pop remains one of the most popular coaches in football history. When a thirty-two-cent stamp honoring him was unveiled in 1996, S. David Fineman, governor of the United States Postal Service, said, "Pop Warner was an amazing innovator and coach whose memory lives on."[3]

## POP WARNER

BORN: April 5, 1871, Springville, New York.

DIED: September 7, 1954, Palo Alto, California.

COLLEGE: Cornell University.

COLLEGE TEAMS COACHED: University of Georgia, 1895–1896;
Cornell University, 1897–1898, 1904–1906; Carlisle,
1899–1903, 1907–1913; University of Pittsburgh, 1915–1923;
Stanford University, 1924–1932; Temple University, 1933–1938.

HONORS/AWARDS: Led teams to three national titles: 1916, 1918,
1926; College Football Hall of Fame, 1951.

At Carlisle Indian Institute, Warner had the opportunity to coach
sports legend Jim Thorpe. It was Warner who talked Thorpe into
returning to school.

BUD WILKINSON

From 1953 to 1957, Bud Wilkinson's University of Oklahoma team won a record 47 straight games.

# BUD WILKINSON

**WHEN HE WAS A SENIOR** at the University of Minnesota, Charles "Bud" Wilkinson was captain of his school's football and basketball teams. Later, he earned a master's degree in English Education from Syracuse University. To relax, he read classical literature and played the organ. He was a strikingly handsome man with a smooth speaking style. He would have made a great professor or maybe even a movie star. Instead, he became head football coach at the University of Oklahoma in 1947.

Wilkinson's teams were exciting and high scoring. He pioneered the "Go-Go," or no-huddle offense. When his offenses did have a huddle, they sprinted from it to the line of scrimmage.

The Sooners utilized the split T formation and a "run to daylight" offense. "When we run a handoff," Wilkinson explained, "the ball carrier has the option, when he gets the ball, of hitting anywhere from between the guards to outside of the defensive tackle."[1]

But Oklahoma kept the opposing defenses honest by relying on the option play as well. In order to stop the option against his own team, Wilkinson and his assistant, Gomer Jones, came up with a 5–4 defensive alignment, which became known as the "Oklahoma defense."

It was not just his strategy that made Wilkinson successful. "He can inspire you by talking quietly far more than the ranting, raving type," said Billy Vessels, a Sooner halfback.[2]

During the 1950s, Oklahoma was the nation's college football powerhouse. From 1948 to 1958, Wilkinson's teams were 107–8–2. He became the first college football coach to host his own regular television program.

After going 8–3 and winning the Gator Bowl in 1947, the Sooners were undefeated the next season. That was the start of a thirty-one-game winning streak. In 1950, Oklahoma was crowned the national champion.

From 1953 to 1957, Wilkinson's teams won an incredible forty-seven consecutive games. The Sooners again were number one in 1955 and 1956. The 1956 squad scored 466 points.

Wilkinson was winning games, but he was also winning the respect and admiration of his colleagues. "I've only known one genius in my lifetime," said Eddie Crowder, Oklahoma's quarterback in the early 1950s and later the coach at the University of Colorado. "His name was Bud Wilkinson."[3] Ara Parseghian coached against him at Northwestern. "Bud was my idol," he said, "and I felt uncomfortable looking across the field at him when we beat him."[4]

In 1961, President John F. Kennedy appointed Wilkinson director of the National Physical Fitness Council, a job he did during the off-season. Two years later, when he retired from coaching, his record was 145–29–4. During his seventeen years at Oklahoma, his teams had won four Orange Bowls and two Sugar Bowls.

Wilkinson then turned to politics. He ran unsuccessfully for the United States Senate in 1964. Later, he became a White House consultant to President Richard M. Nixon. He returned to football briefly in the late 1970s as coach of the St. Louis Cardinals in the National Football League.

"Bud always looks like he just stepped out of a barber shop," said Bear Bryant. "I wish I had his class."[5]

# BUD WILKINSON

BORN: April 23, 1916, Minneapolis, Minnesota.

DIED: February 9, 1994.

COLLEGE: University of Minnesota.

COLLEGE TEAMS COACHED: University of Oklahoma, 1947–1963.

HONORS/AWARDS: Led teams to three national championships: 1950,
1955, 1956; AFCA Coach of the Year, 1949; College
Football Hall of Fame, 1969.

Wilkinson is among the all-time leaders in winning percentage
and is a member of the College Football Hall of Fame.

**Internet Address**

http://oufans.cwis.net/bud.html

# CHAPTER NOTES

**Paul "Bear" Bryant**

1. Mickey Herskowitz, *The Legend of Bear Bryant* (New York: McGraw-Hill, 1987), p. 41.

2. Keith Dunnavant, *Coach: The Life of Paul "Bear" Bryant* (New York: Simon & Schuster, 1996), p. 21.

3. Herskowitz, p. 20.

4. Ibid., pp. 42–43.

5. Dunnavant, p. 26.

6. Herskowitz, p. 73.

7. Ibid., p. 13.

8. Ibid., p. 2.

**Woody Hayes**

1. Jerry Brondfield, *Woody Hayes and the 100-Yard War* (New York: Random House, 1974), pp. 22–23.

2. Ibid., p. 117.

3. Ibid., p. 296.

4. Ibid., p. 264.

**Tom Osborne**

1. Sally Jenkins, "The Quiet Man," *Sports Illustrated*, January 3, 1994, p. 37.

2. Dan Le Batard, "Osborne Earns Title He Always Deserved: Champion," Knight Ridder/Tribune Service, January 2, 1995, on-line.

3. Jenkins, p. 38.

4. Le Batard.

5. Steve Marantz, "The Silent Plainsman," *The Sporting News*, December 19, 1994, on-line.

6. Associated Press dispatch, December 11, 1997.

**Joe Paterno**

1. Dan Jenkins, "The Idea Is to Have Some Fun—And Who Needs to Be No. 1," *Sports Illustrated*, November 11, 1968, p. xx.

2. Mervin D. Hyman and Gordon S. White, Jr., *Joe Paterno: "Football My Way,"* (New York: Macmillan Company, 1971), p. 27.

3. Joe Paterno, *Paterno by the Book* (New York: Random House, 1989), p. 231.

4. Ibid., p. 261.

5. Charles Moritz, ed., *Current Biography Yearbook* (New York: H. W. Wilson, 1984), p. 315.

**Eddie Robinson**

1. Walter Roessing, "Eddie Robinson: A Living Legend," *Boys' Life*, October 1996, on-line.

2. Ibid.

3. Dave Kindred, "There's No Quit in Eddie Robinson," *The Sporting News*, December 23, 1996, on-line.

4. Bill Minutaglio, "He Could Stop Time . . . but not Anymore," *The Sporting News*, August 25, 1997, on-line.

5. "400 Victories and Still Counting," *Ebony*, December 1995, vol. 51, pp. 124–26.

6. Associated Press Dispatch, November 29, 1997.

**Knute Rockne**

1. Jerry Brondfield, *Rockne* (New York: Random House, 1976), p. 6.

2. Allison Danzig, *Oh, How They Played the Game* (New York: Macmillan Company, 1971), p. 255.

3. Brondfield, p. 176.

4. Ibid., p. 220.

5. Murray Sperber, *Shake Down the Thunder* (New York: Henry Holt, 1993), p. 240.

**Amos Alonzo Stagg**

1. John Underwood, "A Century of Honesty," *Sports Illustrated*, August 29, 1994, p. 99.

2. Ibid.

3. Amos Alonzo Stagg, as told to Wesley Winans Stout, *Touchdown!* (New York: Longmans, Green, and Company, 1927), p. 302.

**Barry Switzer**

1. Barry Switzer with Bud Shrake, *Bootlegger's Boy* (New York: William Morrow, 1990), p. 102.

2. Ibid., p. 117.

3. Ibid., p. 140.

4. Ibid., p. 29.

**Pop Warner**

1. John Durant and Les Etter, *Highlights of College Football* (New York: Hastings House Publishers, 1970), p. 107.

2. Art Berke, ed., *Lincoln Library of Sports Champions*, vol. 18 (Columbus, Ohio: Frontier Press Company, 1985), p. 116.

3. "Pop Warner to Be Honored on 1997 Postage Stamp," United States Postal Service release, November 2, 1996.

**Bud Wilkinson**

1. Ralph Hickok, *A Who's Who of Sports Champions* (Boston: Hougton Mifflin, 1995), p. 841.

2. John Durant and Les Etter, *Highlights of College Football* (New York: Hastings House Publishers, 1970), p. 165.

3. "A Winner, a Teacher," *Sports Illustrated*, February 21, 1994, on-line.

4. Bill Connors, "Bud Beat Them All, Sooner or Later," *The Sporting News*, February 21, 1994, on-line.

5. Ibid.

# INDEX